...ling 0118 9015950
0118 9015100

Creepy Creatures

Mosquitoes

Sue Barraclough

Heinemann
LIBRARY

Little Nippers

www.heinemann.co.uk/library
Visit our website to find out more information about **Heinemann Library** books.

To order:
☎ Phone 44 (0) 1865 888066
🖹 Send a fax to 44 (0) 1865 314091
💻 Visit the Heinemann Bookshop at www.heinemann.co.uk/library to browse our catalogue and order online.

First published in Great Britain by Heinemann Library, Halley Court, Jordan Hill, Oxford OX2 8EJ, part of Harcourt Education.
Heinemann is a registered trademark of Harcourt Education Ltd.

Editorial: Sarah Shannon and Louise Galpine
Design: Jo Hinton-Malivoire and bigtop, Bicester, UK
Picture Research: Hannah Taylor and Sally Claxton
Production: Camilla Smith

Originated by Dot Gradations
Printed and bound in China by South China Printing Company

ISBN 0 431 93259 X (hardback)
09 08 07 06 05
10 9 8 7 6 5 4 3 2 1

ISBN 0 431 93264 6 (paperback)
09 08 07 06 05
10 9 8 7 6 5 4 3 2 1

British Library Cataloguing in Publication Data
Barraclough, Sue
595.7'72
Creepy Creatures: Mosquitoes
A full catalogue record for this book is available from the British Library.

Acknowledgements
The publishers would like to thank the following for permission to reproduce photographs: Alamy Images pp. 8-9 (22DigiTal), 4 (Fogstock), 7top 7bottom (Holt Studios International Ltd),13 (NaturePicks), 21 (Roger Eritja), 18 (Wildimages); Ardea p. 6 (Steve Hopkin); Bubbles p. 23; Corbis pp.10-11 (CDC/PHIL), 5 (Pat O'Hara); FLPA p.14 (David T. Grewcock); Garden Matters p. 22 (M Collins); Holt Studios International Ltd p.12; NHPA pp. 19, 20 (George Bernard); Science Photo Library pp.17 (Claude Nuridsany & Marie Perennou), 15 (Darwin Dale), 16 (David M. Schlesier).

Cover photograph of a mosquito reproduced with permission Corbis/ CDC/ PHIL.

Every effort has been made to contact copyright holders of any material reproduced in this book. Any omissions will be rectified in subsequent printings if notice is given to the publishers.

The paper used to print this book comes from sustainable resources.

Contents

Mosquitoes

Mosquitoes are tiny flies. Some are so tiny, they are difficult to see.

You need a magnifying glass to see a mosquito clearly.

Different mosquitoes

Gnats and midges belong to the same family as mosquitoes.

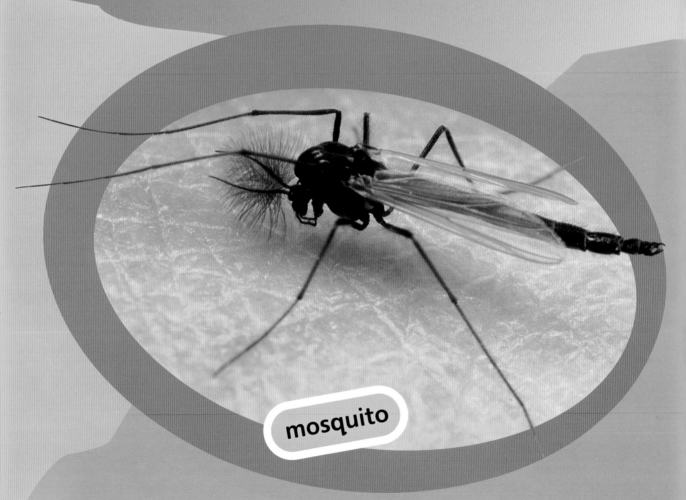

mosquito

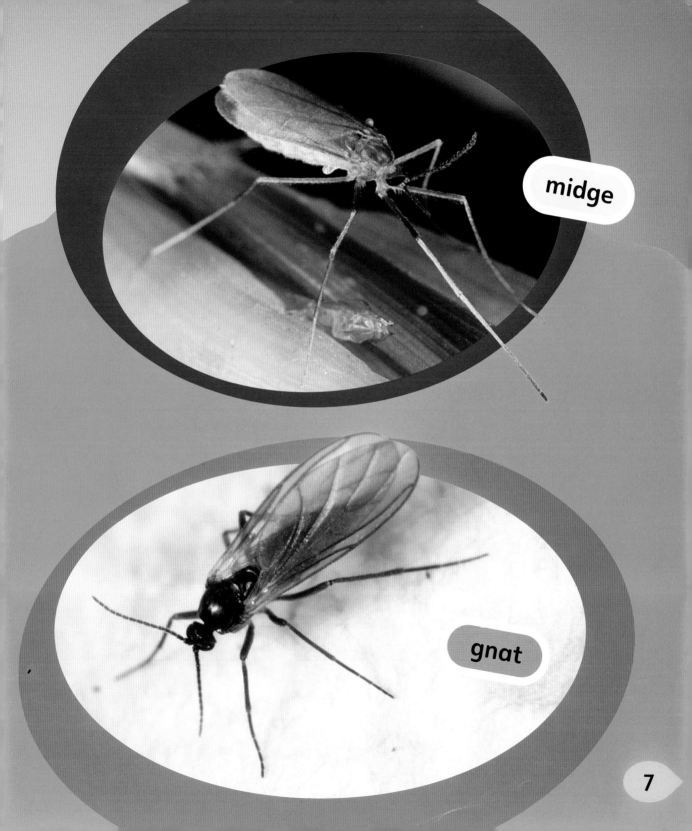

midge

gnat

Looking for mosquitoes

Mosquitoes live near
ponds and ditches.

You might
see them on
a summer
evening.

A mosquito's body

Mosquitoes are insects.
Their bodies have
three parts.

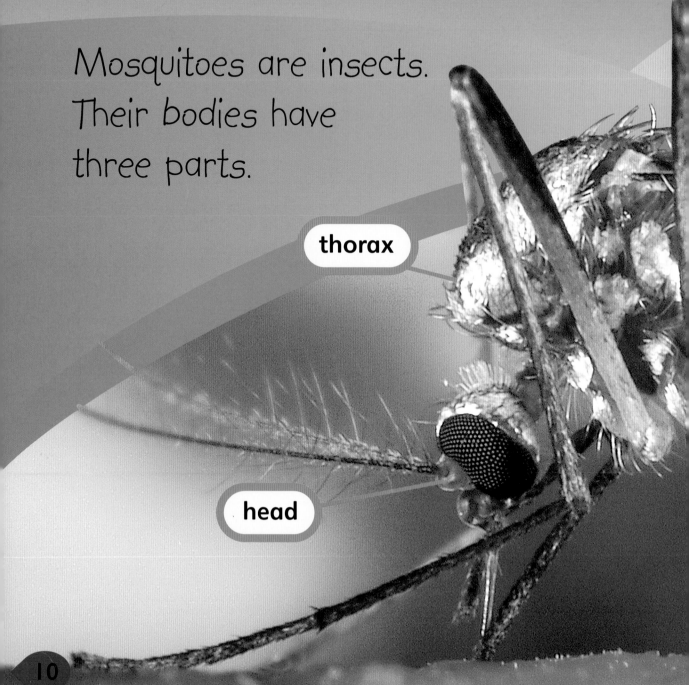

thorax

head

They have six long legs.
How many can you count?

abdomen

A mosquito's head

A mosquito has very **sharp** mouthparts for piercing and sucking.

Slurp, slurp!

Their feather-like antennae are used for touching and smelling.

antennae

Mosquito noises

Mosquitoes make a whining sound as they fly around.

EEEEEEEEEEeeeeeeeeee!

Zzzzzzzzzzzz!

Their wings beat so fast that they make a noise.

A mosquito's eggs

A female mosquito lays hundreds of eggs on still water.

She lays them in groups that f l o a t together.

Growing and changing

The egg changes into a larva that **wriggles** in the water.

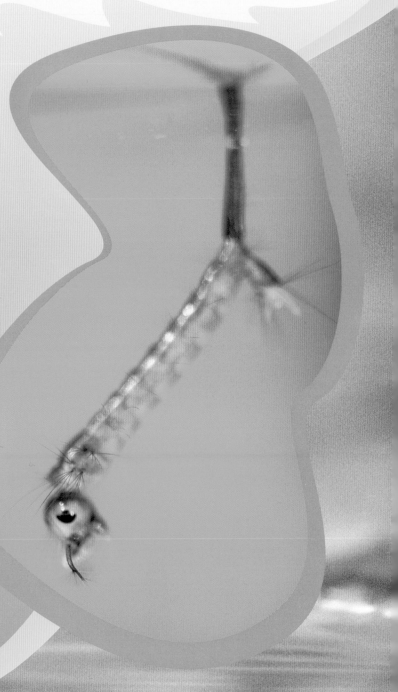

Finally, the adult mosquito waits for its wings to dry. Then it can fly away.

Food for mosquitoes

Male mosquitoes eat nectar, which they suck from flowers.

Females eat blood, which they suck from animals.

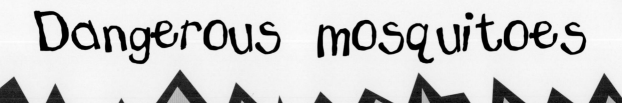

Dangerous mosquitoes

When mosquitoes suck blood from people they can spread diseases.

Ouch!

There are creams
to help if you
are bitten.

Index

Notes for adults

This series supports the young child's exploration of their learning environment and their knowledge and understanding of their world. The four books when used together will enable comparison of similarities and differences to be made. (N.B. Many of the photographs in **Creepy Creatures** show the creatures much larger than life size. The first spread of each title shows the creature at approximately its real life size.)

The following Early Learning Goals are relevant to the series:
• Find out about, and identify, some features of living things, objects, and events that they observe
• Ask questions about why things happen and how things work
• Observe, find out about, and identify features in the place they live and the natural world
• Find out about their local environment and talk about those features they like and dislike.

The books will help the child extend their vocabulary, as they will hear new words. Since words are used in context in the book this should enable the young child gradually to incorporate them into their own vocabulary. Some of the words that may be new to them in **Mosquitoes** are *thorax, abdomen, mouthparts, antennae, larva, nectar* and *diseases*.

The following additional information may be of interest:
Mosquitoes are tiny and delicate, but they are one of the most dangerous blood-sucking insects. In some tropical countries, female mosquitoes can spread diseases such as malaria, and they are the cause of millions of deaths every year. Mosquitoes feed mostly at dusk or during the night. Female mosquitoes need a meal of blood because this provides proteins necessary for the development of their eggs. Some mosquito breeding grounds can be treated with insecticides, and draining and filling of ponds and ditches is sometimes carried out as a more permanent solution. However, these methods of control may cause pollution and other environmental damage.

Follow-up activities
Children might like to follow up what they have learned about mosquitoes by making their own observations in parks and gardens. Develop ideas and understanding by discussing any features they find interesting, and encourage children to record their observations and ideas in drawings, paintings, or writing.